NORTH EASTERN RENAISSANCE

Andrew Scott

TWENTY-FIVE YEARS OF STEAM LOCOMOTIVE
PRESERVATION IN NORTH EAST ENGLAND

LONDON
IAN ALLAN LTD

Published by Ian Allan Ltd for the North Eastern
Locomotive Preservation Group,
57 Millview Drive, Tynemouth, NE30 2QD.

First published 1991

ISBN 0 7110 2023 X

Printed by Ian Allan Printing Ltd at their works at
Coombelands, Runnymede, England.

Design & artwork by Robert Wilcockson

CONTENTS

ACKNOWLEDGEMENTS

This book would not have been produced without the help of John Hunt
and Maurice Burns who made many
helpful suggestions on the text and
who produced the photographs. But
there would have been no book to produce if it had not been for the large
number of volunteers over the last 25
years who have worked against the
odds to create a North Eastern
Renaissance. This book is dedicated to
them.

Front cover: **On 13 January 1991 No 2392 makes a
fine sight as it heads the 13.00 Grosmont-
Goathland on a crisp winter's day.**
Peter J. Robinson

Rear cover, top: **2005 coasts alongside Loch Eilt
with a Fort William-Mallaig train in August 1987.**
Maurice Burns

Rear cover, bottom left: **901 rounds Beckhole
curve with its first test train following restoration, 16 September 1990.**
Maurice Burns

Rear cover, bottom right: **60019 masquerading as
2509 Silver Link stands outside the workshop at
ICI Wilton in June 1988.** *John Hunt*

INTRODUCTION

The north east of England was the birthplace of steam railways. Here, men like William Hedley and George Stephenson built the world's first locomotives in the opening years of the 19th century. Their job was to haul trains of coal from the collieries down to the banks of the Tyne, Wear and Tees where it could be loaded into ships.

The steam locomotive went on to provide transport for the world. Yet 150 years later, as the end of the steam era approached, some of the last steam locos in Britain were still to be found at work serving the collieries of Tyne and Wear.

In September 1967 British Railways extinguished the fires in the last of its engines in the north east. Steam engines were replaced by diesels at such depots as Tyne Dock, Sunderland and Hartlepool. Less than a year later, British Railways had withdrawn its last steam locomotive from service and the entire network was given over to diesel and electric power.

That the thrill of seeing and hearing a steam loco hard at work can still be experienced is thanks largely to groups of volunteers who worked to save and restore these superb machines for posterity.

In the north east, there was something particularly special about those final days of steam. Maybe it was the feeling of continuity from the days of the railway pioneers. Perhaps it was because many of the surviving locomotives in that area had themselves been part of the scene for so long. Many of them were more than 50 years old. By 1967 they were the oldest engines still at work on BR, still providing the unglamorous yet essential service for which they had been designed so many years before.

Amongst the enthusiasts who gathered at the lineside in those final months of north east steam operation, were some who felt that it was worth trying to save something of this part of our industrial heritage. In late 1966, in a dingy room above a pub just outside Newcastle's Central Station, they organised themselves into an organisation with the unwieldy but self explanatory title of the North Eastern Locomotive Preservation Group. At this first meeting, with little idea of how it was to be achieved, they resolved to attempt to purchase a locomotive!

From these inauspicious beginnings has emerged a charitable trust which, 25 years later, owns four locomotives, manages three others and has played a major part in the preservation of several more. Its locomotives have operated not just at its base on the North Yorkshire Moors Railway but also at locations as far apart as Somerset and the West Highlands of Scotland.

The chapters which follow aim to give a flavour of the work and achievements of this remarkable group of volunteers – the North Eastern Locomotive Preservation Group.

1 STEAM IN THE NORTH EAST

Most of the locos that have been in NELPG's care have spent all or part of their working lives hauling coal from the north east's pits. It was for just this job that a network of waggonways was developed from the 17th century onwards. Some of the routes regularly traversed by these successors to those early horse drawn wagons had been in use since the early 18th century. The 0-6-0 and 0-8-0 mineral locos operated by the Group can be seen as direct descendants of the early locomotives built by William Hedley and, above all, by George Stephenson.

During the 19th century, a dense network of railways developed in Northumberland, Durham and the Cleveland area of north Yorkshire to serve industry and the communities associated with it. Hundreds of coal mines and scores of quarries supplied the raw materials for the north east's

steelworks, factories and power stations. Coal in vast quantities was taken by sea from ports on the area's river estuaries to fuel industry at home and abroad. The North Eastern Railway provided the arteries of this enterprise.

The North Eastern Railway had come into existence in 1854 when several companies combined to form a system based on a main line from Leeds to Berwick upon Tweed. In 1863 even the pioneering Stockton and Darlington Railway had joined the group. By 1874, with the absorption of the Blyth and Tyne Railway, the North Eastern had achieved a virtual monopoly of railway services in north east England; a contrast to the intense competition which was to be found in most other densely populated areas.

The only other railways of note were the private systems operated by several of the larger colliery companies. Some of these systems, particularly those

around Ashington, Hetton and Philadelphia remained active into the 1980s.

The North Eastern Railway's requirements for its coal and mineral engines were straightforward – no nonsense power and lots of it! By the time of World War 1 these requirements were being met by two distinct types of loco – six and eight-coupled tender engines, examples of which were to survive until the end of BR steam operations in the area. The North Eastern Locomotive Preservation Group was formed in 1966 to preserve an example of each. It is these which were to form the basis of the Group's collection.

The 'P3' (referred to by the LNER and BR as Class J27) was the final development of a series of 0-6-0s with small wheels and ever-increasing sized boilers. These were ideal for the relatively low speeds and short distances covered by much of the company's col

liery traffic. They were designed by Wilson Worsdell, the North Eastern Railway's Chief Mechanical Engineer and were introduced in 1906.

The huge, 5ft 6in diameter boiler applied to the 'P3' and its predecessor, the 'P2' was a major innovation and was the key to the locomotive's ability to handle heavy loads of coal on the company's steeply graded routes. More than 100 of Class P3 were built and the type was to be a familiar sight in the north east for more than 60 years. BR No 65894 (NER No 2392), the last to be built, was selected by NELPG members as the first target of their fund raising and was purchased soon after its withdrawal in September 1967.

In parallel with its need for an 0-6-0, the North Eastern Railway had a requirement for a larger engine for its heavier and longer distance mineral trains. This was met by a series of two-cylinder 0-8-0 designs and in 1913, Vincent Raven, Wilson Worsdell's successor, introduced his version, designated Class T2 (LNER Class Q6). 120 of these impressive and successful engines were built and formed an essential part of the north eastern railway scene until 1967.

Once the 'P3' had been successfully purchased, fund raising continued in order to save the last surviving 'T2', No 2238 (BR No 63395). Time was not on the group's side but eventually the engine was saved. After restoration it became the first of NELPG's locomotives to start a new career hauling trains on the North Yorkshire Moors Railway.

As traffic continued to grow the North Eastern Railway predicted a need for an even larger freight locomotive. In 1919 Raven produced a three-cylinder 0-8-0 of immense power derived from his successful Class Z

Atlantic express engines. The railway operators had only limited need for such power and only 15 of Class T3 (LNER Class Q7) were to be produced. They served the railway best on one of the toughest tasks in the area, hauling iron ore trains from Tyne Dock to Consett, 1,000ft above sea level. On the steepest gradients (as much as 1 in 35 in places), 'Q7s' were to be found at both front and rear of 700ton trains.

As the final development of NER freight power, No 901 (BR No 63460), the prototype, was selected by BR for the national collection of preserved locomotives. It is now owned by the National Railway Museum who placed the engine in the care of NELPG in 1979. The Group has subsequently restored 901 to working order.

At the other end of the motive power scale were the vast numbers of 0-6-0T shunting locomotives employed in goods yards and at coal staithes all over the North Eastern Railway system. In 1982, NELPG was able to purchase the last survivor of these locomotives, Class J72 (NER Class E1) No 69023. Class E1 was introduced by Wilson Worsdell in 1898, yet 69023 was not built until more than 50 years later, in 1951. It is a remarkable testimony to the soundness of the original design that on four occasions in the first half of the 20th century when new engines were required for this type of duty, more of this same 19th century design were

Left: These two photos, although similar, are valuable records of NELPG engines in action between the wars. The first *(above left)* shows 901, the pioneer member of Class Q7. When introduced in 1919 these three-cylinder engines were some of the most powerful freight locomotives to be seen. 901 was added to the National Collection on its withdrawal in 1962 and became, therefore, part of the National Railway Museum's collection when that museum was set up in the 1970s. Today it is on loan to NELPG who have restored the engine to running order, completing the work in 1990. It is seen here heading down the east coast main line near Cowton hauling a heavy mineral train. As the prototype of its class, pictures of 901 in its early years are not uncommon. NELPG's 2238, on the other hand, a much more mundane member of Class Q6, was photographed only rarely. This picture, *(centre left)* taken sometime in the 1920s shows 2238 passing West Wylam Junction with a train from the Carlisle line.

The engine survived as BR No 63395 until the end of steam in the north east and was stored for preservation. In the end, its survival depended on a happy chance. The steep rise in copper prices precipitated by Rhodesia's unilateral declaration of independence led BR to sell the loco for scrap with no warning to the Group. However, the driver detailed to take the loco to the scrapyard was somehow unavoidably absent from work after a particularly successful evening's drinking. The 24 hours thus gained enabled the Group to negotiate a new deal and the engine was saved for posterity!

W. Rogerson; J.W. Armstrong

Right: **69023 was one of that extraordinary group of Class J72 built between 1949 and 1951 to a design that was already more than 50 years old. Several of this final batch spent part of their relatively short careers at Blaydon depot. Here NELPG's engine is seen in the Blaydon roundhouse, totally dwarfed by its two Class Q7 neighbours.**

69023 was to lead a charmed existence. Following the demise of the rest of the class by 1964, it was one of two which survived in departmental use, to provide steam for unfreezing frozen wagons and points. This lease of life led to its purchase for preservation in 1966 by Ron Ainsworth, who housed it at first on the Keighley & Worth Valley Railway. Here it hauled some of the line's earliest trains. Later it provided all of the motive power for the Derwent Valley Railway's short-lived experiment with steam passenger services. With the help of a Science Museum grant, NELPG bought the engine from Mr Ainsworth's family in 1982. Ron Ainsworth had named the engine Joem, after his parents. The name has stuck, despite the removal of the nameplate to the interior of the loco's cab during its 1987 overhaul.
Alan Blencowe

built. The last few must have made a strange contrast in Darlington Works alongside the up to date Ivatt 2-6-0s being produced at the same time.

Away from the mundane world of mineral traffic, the north east also saw its share of the more glamorous world of main line steam expresses. In the 1930s, competition between the west and east coast routes to Scotland led the London and North Eastern Railway's engineer, Nigel Gresley, to produce a streamlined development of his successful pacific express locomotives. The 'A4s' were to handle many of the crack east coast expresses for the next 25 years, until the advent of diesel power. The first of this type was No

2509 Silver Link which was produced to haul the new Silver Jubilee streamlined express between London and Newcastle in 1935. Subsequent batches included a series named after birds and allocated to more general express duties. Mallard, of course, was to become world famous when it broke the world speed record for steam traction in 1938. Another of this series, No 4464 Bittern (BR No 60019) is now in NELPG's care, on long term loan from its owner, NELPG Vice-President Geoff Drury. This engine has been

Above: A British Railways policy decision at the end of 1962 saw the withdrawal of the entire 'Q7' class. Presumably, retention of 15 examples of a non-standard type could not be justified in the face of falling traffic and the availability of more modern types. As the prototype, 63460 was earmarked for the National Collection and appeared on two special workings before finally disappearing into storage. Here she is seen heading an enthusiast tour of north eastern mineral lines in September 1963. The train is passing Consett motive power depot where two 'Q6' 0-8-0s were resting between duties. *N. Skinner*

Left: Sunderland remained a busy centre right to the end of north eastern steam operations. Both 63395 and 65894 saw out their final days moving coal from local collieries to power stations and the coastal ports. One of the most spectacular sights was the regular ascent of empty wagon trains up Seaton Bank to the collieries around Hetton. This 1 in 45 incline had originally been cable hauled. 63395 is seen here on just such a duty in that final summer of 1967.
A.R. Thompson

restored to its original appearance with fairings enclosing its driving wheels but has been repainted to represent Silver Link, that locomotive having been scrapped in the 1960s. The distinctive appearance of this silver streamliner forms an evocative

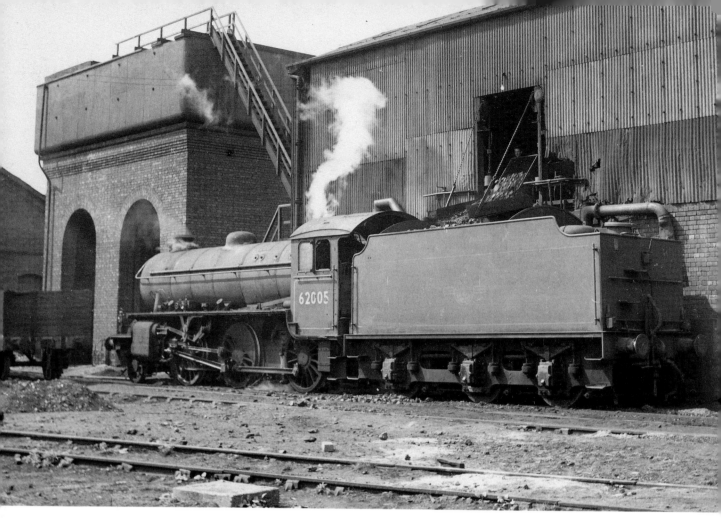

Above: **62005**'s career, perhaps not surprisingly for a mixed traffic loco, had been much more varied than that of the 'J27' and 'Q6'. It was built in 1949 and in its earlier years the engine worked trains as diverse as holiday specials to Blackpool and main line freights to London, from its home bases at Darlington, Heaton and Ardsley, near Wakefield. But with the advent of diesel power 62005 was relegated to more mundane duties and it finished its BR service operating coal trains around Blyth. The engine is seen here at the coaling stage at North Blyth shed in June 1966. *John Hunt*

Right: **62005**'s unglamorous latter years were brightened a little by its use for royal and special train duties. Twice the engine was employed to haul the Queen's train during visits to the north east. Its use on railtours included the 'Whitby Moors' tour, the last steam passenger train in BR days over what is now the North Yorkshire Moors line. In May 1967, 62005 headed the 'Three Dales Railtour' which visited branch lines in Wensleydale, Swaledale and Weardale. Here, the 'K1' is seen heading up Weardale from Stanhope. Later it was to spend several years in store before being donated to **NELPG** in 1972. *Maurice Burns*

elow: Alone amongst the engines with which ~~~e Group has had close involvement, 44767 has ~~w direct connections with the north east. 44767 ~~as built as a unique variant of Stanier's well ~~~own Class 5. It was turned out in 1947 with ~~~~ephenson valve gear to its outside cylinders, giving the engine a very distinctive appearance when seen in action. After spending most of its career in Lancashire, 4767 was latterly based at Kingmoor depot in Carlisle. Here, with its reputation for dogged rather than speedy performance, it was frequently used on the faster freight and parcels trains on the hilly routes to the north and south of Carlisle. In March 1967, the photographer caught 44767 nearing Ais Gill Summit on the Settle and Carlisle line with a freight train. The bleak outline of Wild Boar Fell looms in the background.

44767 had been privately purchased from BR in 1968. However, little had been done towards its restoration by the time Ian Storey, then NELPG's chairman, bought the engine in 1974. *Brian Stephenson*

Bottom: Although most enthusiasts' attention was centred on BR steam, as this disappeared interest grew in the National Coal Board's operations. The former Lambton, Hetton and Joicey Railway, based around Philadelphia in mid-Durham, was the doyen of north-eastern systems. Not only did the LHJR's trains operate over BR's own lines as well as its own substantial (and fully signalled) network but it also operated locos far bigger than most colliery shunters. The last tender engines had disappeared at the end of the 1950s but powerful 0-6-2Ts continued in service until the end of steam on the system in February 1969. Two of these were purchased by NELPG and NYMR members and they have continued their careers on the North Yorkshire Moors Railway. No 5, built by Robert Stephenson and Co in 1909, is seen here storming through Philadelphia on a train from Herrington Colliery to Penshaw exchange sidings in January 1969. Alongside, No 29, built by Kitson & Co of Leeds in 1904, is prepared for its next duty. *I.S. Carr*

reminder of the pinnacle of British express train operation in the days before car and airline competition.

After the last war the engineer A.H. Peppercorn was responsible for the LNER's last new steam engine designs. Nationalisation took place in 1948 and BR's own designs were to be produced for a few years before diesel power swept away the steam locomotive from Britain's railways. Two of Peppercorn's locomotives are to be found in NELPG's collection.

No 60532 Blue Peter represents the final development of the LNER Pacific. With smaller wheels than the 'A4s', the engines were not as speedy as their predecessors but they were nevertheless capable of generating immense power. The 'A2s' were to be found on east coast main line expresses along-side the 'A4s' but perhaps are best remembered for their work in Scotland. Both types were to end their days on services between Glasgow, Edinburgh and Aberdeen. Blue Peter is also on long term loan to the Group from its owner, Geoff Drury.

The other Peppercorn locomotive preserved by NELPG is Class K1 No 62005 (preserved as LNER No 2005 although the engine never bore this number in BR service). This was the third engine to come into NELPG ownership when it was donated by supporters of the Group in 1972.

These small wheeled 2-6-0s were designed nominally as replacements for locomotives like the 'J27' but were capable of far higher speeds and were regarded as mixed traffic engines. In the north east, particularly towards the end of steam operations, most of their work was on mineral trains. Others had regularly worked short distance expresses in East Anglia and passenger trains on the West Highland line from

Above: **In 1986, NELPG took on the responsibility for two locomotives of a very different type – the London and North Eastern Railway main line Pacific locomotives Bittern and Blue Peter. Bittern, designed by Nigel Gresley and a Class A4 from the same batch as the steam speed record holder Mallard, was a common sight in the north east for many years on Kings Cross-Edinburgh main line expresses. In this scene from 1939, the one year old Bittern is seen accelerating through Low Fell station in Gateshead with a Sunday Newcastle-King's Cross express.** *W. Bryce Greenfield*

Above right: **Nearly 30 years later, the 'A4s' were seeing out their days on the Glasgow to Aberdeen run. By now numbered 60019, Bittern is seen here leaving Gleneagles on the 1.30pm Aberdeen to Glasgow express in the winter of 1965. The change in the engine's appearance resulting from the wartime removal of wheel-fairings can clearly be seen in these photographs.** *Paul Riley*

Right: **Blue Peter started its career in 1948 working express trains on the east coast main line, based at York. Before long, though, it moved to Scotland where it spent much of the rest of its career working expresses between Glasgow, Edinburgh and Aberdeen. Here it is seen leaving Stirling with an Aberdeen-Glasgow express in July 1966.** *Maurice Burns*

Glasgow to Fort William and Mallaig. In preservation, of course, the engine was to visit those far flung highland routes but that is a story for a later chapter!

The days when steam was seen in everyday use on British Railways or even on the National Coal Board's private systems are now becoming just a distant memory. The photographs which follow set out to recall the spectacle of NELPG's locos at work in the days before their preservation.

2 TYNE DOCK TO SHILDON

When NELPG acquired its first locos, they were housed in the semi-derelict remains of the wagon works adjacent to the old Tyne Dock steam depot between South Shields and Jarrow. Here the first working parties embarked on the task of preparing the engines for their new life in preservation. But it was clear that a new home was needed as the Tyne Dock workshop was earmarked for early demolition.

Finding a permanent home for its growing collection was a major issue in the early days. At the beginning of 1967, the Keighley and Worth Valley Railway was the only preservation scheme in the north of England. But soon, news of a plan to save the North Eastern Railway line from Grosmont towards Pickering was received. Here would be the ideal home for the Group's NER engines.

Although the North Yorkshire Moors Railway Preservation Society was given access to its line in November 1968, it was out of the question for NELPG's engines to be moved there immediately. The only covered accommodation was Grosmont tunnel and maintenance facilities were non-existent. The Group's short term aim had to be to find a temporary home where restoration work could take place, whilst accumulating the equipment needed to establish a maintenance facility at Grosmont. In the end, it was the massive but little used roundhouse at BR's Thornaby motive power depot which was to provide a temporary home for the Group's working parties until Grosmont was sufficiently developed.

In 1970 the NYMR was able to start running a service for members only and this continued until the official reopening of the line in 1973. By this time, 'P3' No 2392, 'T2' No 2238 and the two Lambton tank locomotives, Nos 5 and 29, were all based at Grosmont. In 1974 the 'K1' No 2005 was to join them.

As the 1970s unfolded, NELPG was settling into a new routine providing motive power for the NYMR. But

events in 1975 were to prove a watershed.

NELPG had been closely involved in the plans for events to celebrate the 150th anniversary of the opening of the Stockton and Darlington Railway. The Group's engines were to play a starring role in the August 1975 Shildon exhibition and the ancillary events were to give NELPG its first taste of operations on the main line. The success of commercial activities in 1975 – railtours and sales stalls at Stockton and Darlington Railway anniversary events – encouraged members to start planning for the Group's own depot at Grosmont.

Nine years of hard work, culminating in the Shildon celebrations, had turned the North Eastern Locomotive Preservation Group into one of the steam preservation world's most effective operators. The events of 1975 were to set the agenda for the Group's second decade.

Above: **Whilst all this was going on at Thornaby, the North Yorkshire Moors Railway's negotiations to take over its line were proceeding well. Permission was received to operate members' special trains from the summer of 1970 and the completed 'Q6', together with No 29 were moved to the line in June. No 29 heads a packed special train at Ellerbeck in July 1970. The train consists of all of the NYMR's operational coaching stock at that time: two Thompson coaches and the Hull and Barnsley Railway brake.** *Peter J. Robinson*

Above right: **65894's restoration took another year and it was not until October 1971 that the engine arrived at Grosmont from its restoration on Teesside. However a thorough job had been done, as this picture taken at its handing over ceremony shows. The engine was repainted in North Eastern Railway goods livery; black, lined out in red and carrying the NER's distinctive oval brass numberplates. Comparison with the photo on page 4 will show some of the changes made to the locomotive during its restoration. The tender had been swapped for a more typical standard version in better condition. The dome cover, too, was swapped for an earlier type. Other changes were necessary to make the engine suitable for passenger haulage. Neither the 'Q6' nor the 'J27' had ever been fitted with vacuum brake or anything more sophisticated than a three-link coupling. For their new lives as passenger engines it was necessary to provide vacuum brake equipment and screw couplings. It was also decided to fit steam heating equipment. These changes inevitably had some effect on the appearance of the engines but great efforts were made to hide as much of the additional pipework as possible.** *John Hunt*

Left: **In November 1971, NELPG's fifth birthday celebrations were made memorable by a snowfall which brought scenes like this to the NYMR for the first time. The 'Q6' worked special trains for members and is seen here entering the 1 in 49 gradient of the deviation route at Esk Valley.** *Les Nixon*

Below: **In 1972, not long after the completion of 65894's restoration, the 'K1', 62005, was donated to the Group. The engine had been purchased privately from BR several years earlier as a potential source of a replacement boiler for The Great Marquess. When it was discovered that this would not be needed, its owners decided that passing the engine to NELPG was the best option for its future. The new project was embarked upon with enthusiasm and two years later, in April 1974, the 'K1' was standing on the turntable at Thornaby, in steam for the first time in private ownership.** *Maurice Burns*

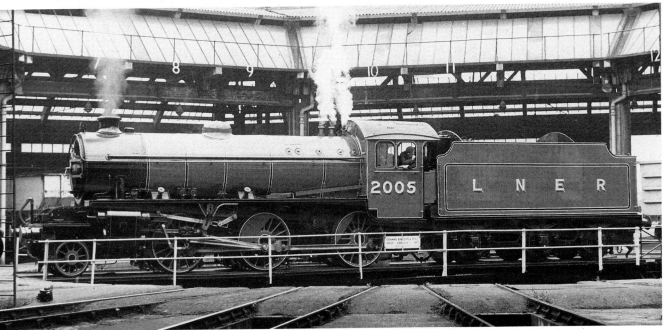

Left: **In 1973, another engine came onto the NELPG scene. 44767, the unique Stephenson valve gear Class 5, was purchased by Ian Storey, then NELPG's Chairman. Along with NELPG's other engines, 4767 was to have a major role to play in the Stockton and Darlington Railway 150th Anniversary celebrations. Yet again, Thornaby was to provide the accommodation for the engine's return to working order and it was delivered straight from that depot to the Shildon celebrations. The Right Hon William Whitelaw (now Lord Whitelaw) was present at Shildon to perform the opening ceremony. In the course of this event, he named the engine, appropriately, George Stephenson. The proud owner is on the left.** *John Hunt*

Above: **It is easy to forget just how spectacular the Shildon celebrations were. When planning commenced, BR's 'steam ban' policy was only just rescinded and the notion of gathering together such a display of preserved steam power seemed like so much moonshine. Yet years of careful preparations led to a most successful event which showed the way for a much more liberal steam operation policy in later years. Early on the morning of the cavalcade, engines are prepared in the yard at Shildon works. The atmosphere of the real life steam depot brought tears to the eye of many a hardened enthusiast.** *John Hunt*

Centre right: **For NELPG, on its home patch and with the only steamable North Eastern Railway locomotives around, the Shildon event was the culmination of nine years of achievement. The Locomotion replica and a National Coal Board Austerity saddle tank symbolic of the coal industry origins of railways headed the procession. Right behind them were NELPG's four locomotives, each in its way acting as a tribute to the north eastern origins of steam railways. To see their four engines lined up together in pride of place confirmed for all involved that NELPG members' hard work over nine years had been worthwhile.** *John Hunt*

Right: **After the event, George Stephenson made straight for Grosmont and service on the NYMR. The Group's own locos spent the autumn back at Thornaby enabling this roundhouse scene to be recorded. After their departure the roundhouse was never again to see use as a restoration depot and it slowly fell into dereliction.** *John Hunt*

3 FROM GROSMONT TO PICKERING

GROSMONT

Left: **1 May 1973 saw the opening of Britain's longest preserved railway line. HRH the Duchess of Kent performed the opening ceremony and is seen here as 2392 and No 29 steam into Grosmont with the empty stock for the reopening special. This was the first royal train to be hauled by preserved steam locomotives and 2392 proudly carried the appropriate four lamp headcode.** *Northern Echo*

Below: **Four years later, Grosmont celebrated the Queen's Silver Jubilee. 29 is seen here leaving Grosmont with a train for Pickering on the rather damp holiday.** *Val Burns*

In June 1967, not long after NELPG's formation, the first meeting was held of the North Yorkshire Moors Railway Preservation Society. Its aim was to preserve the railway from Grosmont, near Whitby, to Ellerbeck, the summit of the line which headed over the moors to Pickering and thence to Malton and York.

The history of the line is rather unusual. In the early 19th century, Whitby's ship owners were still very important players in the seaborne traffic in coal from north eastern ports to London. They looked on with some concern as they saw the economy of rival Stockton bolstered by the Stockton and Darlington Railway in 1825.

Before long, George Stephenson was being requested to report on the potential for a railway to serve Whitby's own hinterland. Here though, the situation was different. The industrial potential of the Yorkshire Moors was low. Between Whitby and Grosmont lay important stone quarries but elsewhere, the freight potential was limited to agricultural materials. Passenger demand too was limited.

Stephenson suggested something very different from the steam railways which were beginning to appear elsewhere; a lightly laid railway which would employ horses to haul single passenger or freight vehicles. The railway would connect Whitby to Pickering and, south of the summit at Ellerbeck, it would exploit the natural gorge of Newtondale – a twisting glacial overflow channel 400ft deep in places, necessitating sharp curves along the line at many points. In a further effort to keep gradients to an acceptable level for the horses, the 300ft difference in level between Beckhole and Goathland was to be overcome by a self-acting cable-hauled incline. There the weight of descending loaded wagons would be employed to raise ascending ones. The line opened in stages in 1835 and 1836 but by 1847 it had been rebuilt as a conventional double track railway connecting Whitby with the Scarborough-York line at Malton. This necessitiated new bridges and a new tunnel at Grosmont. The old one, only large enough for a single line of horse powered railway, is still used as a footpath to the NYMR's loco sheds.

The cable incline remained and it

ESK VALLEY

Above: **The 1976 season was the first time that 2005 and 4767 were to be found together at Grosmont. At Easter, things got off to a good start when the two double-headed one of the first trains of the season. In the distance can be** seen the derelict Deviation Junction signal box, soon to be demolished to make way for NELPG's own engine shed. In the trees below and to the left of the train is the route of George Stephenson's original horse railway. This section survived as a siding to Esk Valley cottages and Beckhole until 1951. *John Hunt*

Right: In days when most passenger trains on the line were no longer than five coaches, the annual visit of the weedkiller train provided the opportunity for freight superpower to show its paces. Apart from the train weight of nearly 400 tons, the weedkilling operation needed the train to operate at a minimum of 25mph. This combination provided quite a challenge for the loco crews. In 1976, NELPG's No 2238 worked the train and is seen here passing Green End, banked by the 'J52' saddle tank, No 1247. *John Hunt*

Below: Fourteen years later at the same spot another 0-8-0 is showing its paces. On 16 September 1990 Class Q7 No 901 undergoes loading tests during a running-in turn before entering service. *Maurice Burns*

Bottom left: During NELPG's 10th anniversary celebrations in October 1976, No 2392 climbs past Esk Valley with a demonstration goods train. *John Hunt*

was not until 1865 that a new deviation line was opened between Grosmont and Moorgates, allowing through steam hauled operation between Whitby and York for the first time. This new section of line contains the section of nearly three miles between Deviation Junction, just outside Grosmont, and Goathland station which rises at a steady gradient of 1 in 49, one of the severest tests of motive power on any preserved railway.

BECKHOLE

Left: **At the NYMR's gala day in October 1987, the newly restored 69023 pilots No 5 on an eight coach train above Beckhole.**

When 69023 was purchased it was soon put into working order but major work was needed before long and overhaul took place at Wilton in 1986/7. Although, the livery was never carried by 69023, it was decided to recreate the green station pilot livery carried by several 'J72s'. Joem's nameplate is now carried inside the cab. *Maurice Burns*

Below: **Back in the days of members' special trains in the early 1970s, No 5 is seen again, only a few hundred yards further up the bank than in the previous shot, with a train of mixed coaches including Thompson and Gresley rolling stock.** *John Hunt*

GOATHLAND

Above: **In spring 1987, 2392 lifts an early season six-coach train away from Goathland bound for Pickering. Bracket signals, the station itself and the autocoach all add to the North Eastern Railway atmosphere.** *Maurice Burns*

Left: **Liveries have always been the subject of spirited debate within NELPG, with decisions on individual locos taken by democratic vote of Group members. For the 'K1', the popular vote has always been for the LNER green livery it would have carried if it had seen the light of day only a couple of years earlier. Nevertheless, for a few months in 1984, in the knowledge that it was soon to be withdrawn for a major overhaul, the opportunity was taken to repaint the engine in 1950s BR livery. Looking authentically dirty, 62005 hurries past Abbots House Farm, south of Goathland, on a train for Pickering.** *John Hunt*

Elsewhere on the line, the gradients are not to be ignored. Between Grosmont and Levisham, a distance of 12 miles, trains must rise and fall around 400ft in each direction.

Also in 1865, a branch was opened from Grosmont up the Esk Valley. This allowed a through service from Whitby to Middlesbrough to be operated,

which today remains as Whitby's only railway link with the rest of the BR network.

For the next hundred years, the Whitby and Pickering line led an uneventful existence. Intermittently, the local ironstone industry boomed and then decayed and for a while Grosmont was the centre of consider-

able industrial activity. Some through passenger services operated to King's Cross and the West Riding but essentially the line was of only local importance.

With the publication of the Beeching report, the line's days were numbered. Whilst the section from Grosmont into Whitby survived as part

MOORGATES

Above: The railway celebrated the Queen's Silver Jubilee in 1977 in fine style. 2238 passes Moorgates on the last lap to the NYMR's summit at Ellerbeck. The front of the 'Q6' is bedecked, perhaps a little incongruously for a mineral engine, with the London, Brighton and South Coast Railway's royal train headboard, on loan for the occasion from the National Railway Museum. *John Hunt*

Right: Skelton Tower, the ruins of a medieval hunting lodge north of Levisham, provides one of the most spectacular views of Newtondale. In May 1977, the 'Q6' is seen from the tower, heading down grade towards Levisham. The eight-coach train was a comparatively rare sight at this time and includes two former King's Cross suburban coaches. These were later sold for use elsewhere as the railway concentrated on corridor stock. *John Hunt*

Below: Generally, NYMR engines face south towards Pickering in order to face uphill on the most daunting of the line's gradients. However, main line outings have provided the opportunity for some engines to come back to the line for short periods facing the 'wrong way'. This has created a whole new range of photographic opportunities as the engines head trains the dozen uphill miles from Pickering to Ellerbeck smokebox first. In the summer of 1976, No 4767 is captured passing Carter's House on the last mile towards Ellerbeck Summit with a train from Pickering. *John Hunt*

of the Esk Valley Line, the route southwards to Malton was to close in 1965.

The North Yorkshire Moors RPS aimed to reopen the railway from Grosmont to the line's summit at Ellerbeck. This was one of many campaigns in the late 1960s to reopen defunct BR lines, many of which were to fall by the wayside. The NYMR's rapid success was due both to the vigour of the preservation society and to the interest of the National Park and the County Council in supporting a scheme which would provide car free access to the superb moorland scenery. As a consequence, a rather hazy plan to see trains eventually running through to Pickering rapidly became a realisable goal.

In November 1968, volunteers were given possession of the route and work could begin on preparing the line for its new role. In July 1970, only three years after that first meeting, the NYMR ran its first passenger trains, albeit for members only, until a light railway order could be obtained.

From that very first day of NYMR passenger operations, NELPG's locos have formed an important part of the NYMR's motive power. The line's steep gradients and 18-mile length demand more of the locomotive fleet than perhaps any other preserved railway and the sheer power of the locos in NELPG's collection has been a major asset to the railway.

More recently, as other main line locos have become available, the pressure on NELPG to provide power has reduced. This has allowed the Group to pursue opportunities for its engines to work further afield. Nevertheless the NYMR remains NELPG's headquarters and for as long as steam remains supreme at Grosmont, you can be sure that NELPG's locos will be taking their turn at the NYMR's challenging gradients.

Since those pioneering days in the early 1970s the NYMR has made steady progress in its plans to create a showpiece steam railway. Despite the setbacks which are inevitable for any enterprise of this kind, each passing year sees improvements in services to the public and in operating facilities. NELPG is proud to have played its part in this story of success.

In this section, we take a trip along the line in the company of the Group's engines.

LEVISHAM

Above: Regular steam services over the most southerly section of the NYMR to Pickering commenced only in 1976, with one steam hauled service each day covering the whole length of the line. Other services were operated by diesel multiple-units. During the spring bank holiday, steam was substituted for broken down diesel units and steam trains passed at Levisham for the first time in many years. That first 'meet' is seen here on 30 May 1976 when No 29, hauling the 'Moorlander' arrives, whilst 2392 with the 'North Yorkshireman' prepares to resume its journey. *John Hunt*

Above left: Like 4767, the 'K1' has also spent periods on the NYMR facing north out of Levisham. Here, 2005 is seen accelerating away from Levisham with a train bound for Grosmont. *John Hunt*

Left: Soon after joining NELPG's stable, in October 1983, the Group ran a special train to thank all those who had had a hand in the acquisition of 69023. In splendid autumn weather, Joem and the NYMR's Great Western saloon are seen here during a run past just north of Levisham. *Peter J. Robinson*

Below: **Levisham is renowned for its authentic North Eastern Railway slotted lower quadrant signals – a type abandoned by most railway companies in the 19th century and yet still common in the north east into the 1960s. George Stephenson is seen here framed by two** such signals as it departs for Pickering in June 1987. By this time the engine had acquired 1950s' BR livery and a Scottish Region style lined out front numberplate to match its shed allocation painted on the bufferbeam. *John Hunt*

KINGTHORPE

Right: **20 years ago, north east England's railways were home to thousand upon thousand of BR's standard 20ton steel hopper coal wagons. Today, they have all but disappeared and a small batch acquired by the NYMR from the private railway system at Rowntree's York chocolate factory are some of the few that survive. During the 1989 NYMR end of season Enthusiast's Weekend, 69023 headed demonstration freight trains including these wagons, evoking something of the North Eastern Railway branch line scene in the process.**

NEW BRIDGE

Above: **4767 seen again during one of its periods facing north. On 2 November 1980, 4767 heads purposefully north from New Bridge Crossing with the last train of the season, the 15.20 for Grosmont.** *Ted Parker*

PICKERING

Left: **Pickering station and the end of the line. 2238 arrives on an unseasonably cold 9 April in 1977 with the inaugural 'North Eastern' through train from Grosmont. The station's North Eastern Railway overall roof had been replaced in BR days by the steel-framed awnings seen here.** *John Hunt*

4 IN THE WORKSHOP

In NELPG's early days, fund raising and the acquisition of locos were the Group's main preoccupations. But with ownership came the need to restore engines to working order and to maintain them to a high standard if they were to operate reliably and safely.

Over the years, the government's Railway Inspectorate, BR's inspectors at Derby and the insurance companies have come to terms with the voluntary preservation movement and the routines of essential maintenance have become established. To keep 70-year old locomotives on the road, however, requires the annual programme to become steadily more ambitious. Today's volunteers regularly undertake, or fund from specialist contractors, work which 20 years ago could only be carried out in railway main workshops.

It did not take long for NELPG's members to realise that buying a locomotive was only the beginning of the story. Premises, equipment, funding and skills were all going to be needed if the Group's engines were to be kept in steam.

Alongside efforts to restore locomotives in temporary accommodation, members scoured the north east for equipment for the permanent workshop which would one day have to be established on the North Yorkshire Moors Railway. All manner of equipment from the smallest special spanner, via machine tools to a 50ton hydraulic locomotive lift was eventually to find its way to Grosmont.

At Grosmont, the first depot building was erected in 1973 and fitted out largely with NELPG equipment. The Group was able to build its own storage shed in the late 1970s and this has been the site of several major overhauls, despite the rather basic working conditions.

By the time its engines arrived on the line, NELPG members had worked on their locos at Tyne Dock, Philadelphia, Hartlepool, Thornaby and ICI Billingham. Thornaby was to

BOILERS

Below: Regulations now require the boiler of a locomotive to be removed every 10 years for a full internal and external examination. Boiler lifts are therefore now seen as part of the routine of running a steam locomotive. In May 1985, the Grosmont steam crane was called in to remove the boiler from the National Railway Museum's 'Q7' 0-8-0 No 63460 at the start of its restoration to running order. *Maurice Burns*

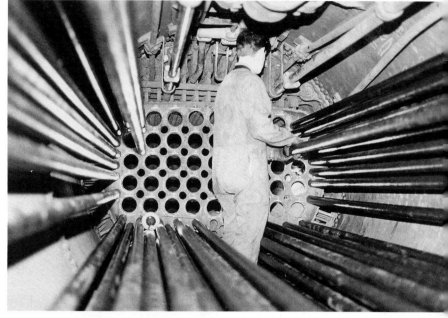

Right: The inside of a loco boiler is full of steel tubes which carry hot gases from the fire to the chimney. These hot gases heat the water that surrounds them in the process. This photo, taken inside Blue Peter's boiler, shows a new set of tubes being fitted. A member of NELPG's volunteer workforce is seen fitting them into the tubeplate which forms the front wall of the firebox. Around the firebox can be seen the narrow waterspace, the sides of which are tied together by a forest of short rods – the stays. These are designed to resist the 250 psi working pressure which would otherwise force the boilerplates apart. *Maurice Burns*

Left: Stays waste away with time and have to be replaced. Here a compressed air tool is being used to remove old stays from the 'K1s' firebox. At the point of contact between hot water, the steel stay and the copper firebox, electrostatic corrosion has wasted the stays to two thirds their original diameter. Maurice Burns

Below: Some weeks later, new stays have been fitted and are ready for riveting over. This view of the top of 2005's boiler shows the outer end of the firebox stays seen above. *Maurice Burns*

Right: **Dismantling boilers and renewing tube plates would have been regarded as out of the question by preservation groups 20 years ago. Today it is almost routine. Here an ICI machinist bores a new tubeplate for the 'J72' No 69023 during its overhaul at Wilton in 1986.** *Maurice Burns*

Below: **Over the years, most of NELPG's engines have needed a new ashpan. These constructions serve the twin purpose of controlling the access of air to the base of the firegrate and of stopping hot ash from spilling out. They were generally made of only thin steel plate and are susceptible to corrosion. On the NYMR and on the West Highland line, it is particularly important to keep ash from bouncing out of the grate and starting lineside fires, so well maintained ashpans are crucial. At 50sq ft, Blue Peter's is the biggest that NELPG has had to reconstruct. This is the new fabrication, ready to be installed beneath the boiler.** *Maurice Burns*

Above: **Smokeboxes too are susceptible to corrosion. That on the 'K1' was replaced during 2005's overhaul at ICI in 1985. Here the new smokebox drum is trial fitted prior to final installation.** *Ted Parker*

Left: **Inside the smokebox, the carefully shaped blastpipe directs the exhaust steam from the cylinders up the chimney. In September 1983, a week before it was due to operate the 'Shildon Shuttle' steam service, the 'K1s' blastpipe was found to be cracked beyond repair. Here, less than 24 hours after the problem was discovered, a patternmaker is seen displaying his art. Working from original LNER drawings and from the damaged original, he was able to produce a pattern from which a new casting could be made. Needless to say, the railtour departed on time!** *Maurice Burns*

have a role until 1975, providing a Teesside location close to the homes of many volunteers for the restoration of locomotives.

A similar role was to be taken in 1984 by a depot in ICI's Wilton works. This was to give rise to a revolutionary improvement in the facilities available to the Group. ICI successively sponsored Community Programme and then Employment Training scheme workers dedicated to working in conjunction with NELPG's volunteers on the restoration of Group locomotives. Taken together with help from ICI's management, the in-house workshop facilities available on the Wilton site and the superb working conditions there, the Wilton project has provided NELPG with one of the most effective restoration centres in the preservation world. Great credit is due to ICI for the long term commitment they have been prepared to make in this unique collaboration between the industrial and voluntary sectors.

NELPG's volunteers found themselves at work in yet another location in 1989 when the 'P3' paid a visit to the Stephenson Railway Museum

CYLINDERS

Below: **65894 was one of the later batch of its class, built with a superheated boiler and piston valves. Earlier engines had the simpler slide valves. Later, its boiler was changed for one of the non-superheated variety but the piston valves remained. In 1984 at the Group's Deviation Shed at Grosmont, valves and cylinders were given a total overhaul whilst the engine's boiler was removed. To improve access to the inside cylinders, the front buffer-beam was also removed, providing an unobstructed view of the massive cylinder casting.** *Mick Roberts*

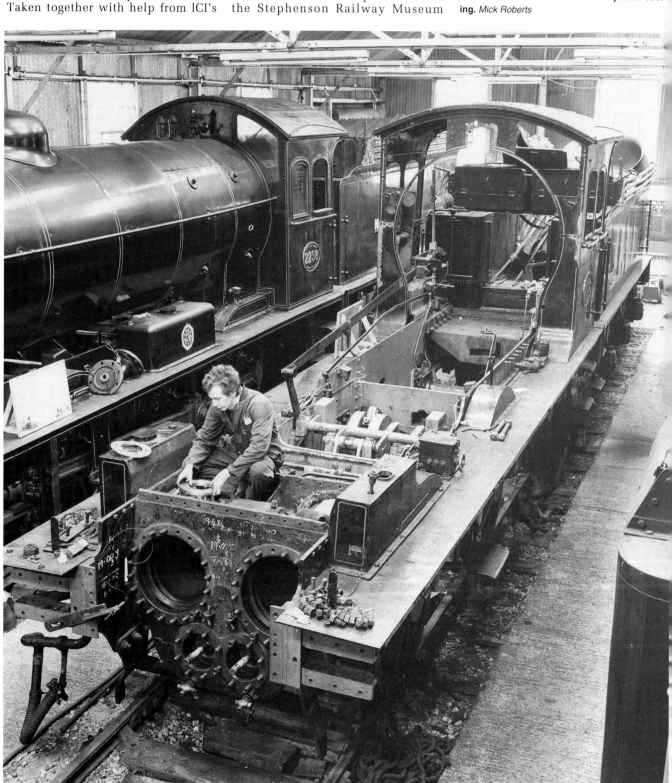

WHEELS AND AXLES

Above: In common with other locos which had experienced a rugged working life, the 'Q7s' axlebox liners were found to be badly worn when it was stripped for restoration. The rigours of a hard life hauling heavy freight trains were compounded by its experiences after withdrawal. It had been towed from Darlington successively to stores at Stratford (East London), Hellifield, Brighton and York before finally moving to Grosmont. Almost undoubtedly, further deterioration took place during this odyssey. In January 1988, during the restoration of the 'Q7', volunteers carried out a trial fitting of the newly overhauled axleboxes into the jacked up frames. *Maurice Burns*

Right: NELPG was one of the first preservation groups to fund the renewal of locomotive tyres when the 'K1' received new tyres in 1981. Locomotive tyres are fitted by heating the new tyre, then letting it cool and shrink into place on the wheel centre. Here, at British Steel's Rotherham works, the new tyre, having been heated on the circular furnace in the background, is lowered into place. At the time, this was the most expensive task that had been undertaken on the Group's locos. Although it absorbed a large percentage of the Group's reserves, it was essential to keeping the engine in service. *Ted Parker*

Left: An alternative approach to gaining access to a locomotive's axleboxes is to lift the engine with a crane. The Grosmont steam crane carries out a spectacular lift of the 'K1' in 1981 during the fitting of the engine's newly retyred wheelsets. *John Hunt*

Right: Careful attention to the condition of wheels and axles is crucial to the safe operation of a steam locomotive and the historic nature of the subject is no inhibition to the use of modern investigation techniques. Before allowing a loco onto its tracks, BR insists that ultrasonic testing of axles is carried out to ensure no dangerous cracks are present. Here, BR technicians carry out ultrasonic tests on Blue Peter's rear driving axle. The apparatus held by the white coated technician is a camera which will record the oscilloscope patterns for retention on Blue Peter's maintenance file. *Maurice Burns*

FINISHING TOUCHES

Centre right: One of the last jobs to be done in the restoration of a locomotive is one of the most skilful. Here, Bittern assumes its new identity as Silver Link and its new number, 2509, at the hands of an expert volunteer signwriter. *Maurice Burns*

ACCOMMODATION

Below: Much of the initial restoration work on NELPG's locos was undertaken in the round-house of Thornaby depot. Opened in 1958, this was the last new steam depot and the last roundhouse built in Britain. By November 1969, when this photo was taken, activity was confined to steam loco restoration and to the repair of wagons. Later it was to fall into total dereliction before finally being demolished in 1988. In this view, 63395 emerges from Thornaby roundhouse on the day of its first steaming in private ownership. *Trevor Ermel*

established in the former Tyne & Wear Metro test track depot in North Tyneside. Here Tyneside members were once again able to work on a Group locomotive without having to travel too far.

But what of the work itself? As experience is gained, the capabilities of members are continually expanding, both in terms of organisation and the practical skills necessary to restore and maintain locomotives. Nearly as important, the money raised by the Group and earned from locomotive operations can be used to purchase the specialist

skills and materials beyond the capabilities of volunteers.

Today, NELPG's management confidently commission from volunteers or contractors work which would have been out of the question 20 years ago. In 1968, renewing the firetubes of a locomotive was seen as a major achievement. By contrast, retubing is now seen as routine. In the last 10 years, apart from a vast amount of routine work, projects have included new tubeplates, smokeboxes and tyres. The 'Q6' has received a completely rebuilt tender, the original having almost

totally rotted away after an eventful 8 year life. Cylinders have been rebored axleboxes totally reconstructed an Blue Peter's sophisticated multi-valv regulator with its multitude of compo nents has been confidentl reconstructed.

Given a continuing ability to attrac funds and, above all, a loyal group o volunteer supporters, the future o NELPG's engines seems assured.

The many components of a locomo tive are only seen in detail when the are fully stripped down for overhau This section looks at some of the man difficult tasks undertaken to keep th show on the road.

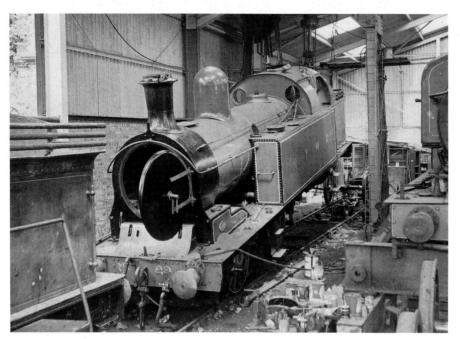

Left: At an early stage in the Group's existence, the need for covered accommodation in which t house and maintain locomotives became apparent. So too was the need for the specialist equipment that had been used by British Railways. The NYMR built its first depot in 1973 and NELPG provided a range of equipment which it had collected. Not least of these was th 50ton capacity set of shearlegs which had formerly served Tweedmouth shed. Here the shearlegs are seen lifting Lambton No 29 into a rather undignified pose for attention to its rear driving wheels. *John Hunt*

Below: An outstandingly successful souvenir sales operation at the Shildon exhibition and profits from railtours provided a substantial boost to NELPG's funds in 1975 and 1976. This was sufficient to allow the purchase of materials for a depot to house NELPG's fleet of locos. The second hand structure was acquired from

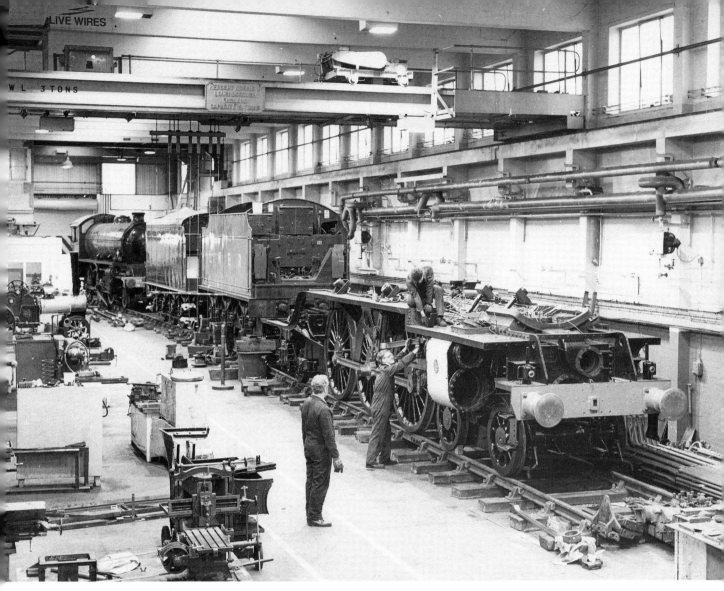

Longmoor, where it had been used as a general store adjacent to the military railway system. Before the building could be brought into use, the derelict Deviation Junction signalbox (see page 19) had to be demolished, several thousand cubic metres of hillside was removed, the building erected and trackwork laid. All of this work was carried out by volunteers. In this 1979 view, rolling stock is being moved under cover into the part completed shed for the first time, before the completion of trackwork. The depot was named Deviation Shed in honour of its location at the point where the 1865 deviation diverged from George Stephenson's original horse railway.
John Hunt

Above: **New standards in accommodation for restoration work were achieved in 1984, when NELPG entered a partnership with ICI at their Wilton works on Teesside. A superbly equipped, centrally heated depot was made available for the use of both NELPG volunteers and an ICI-sponsored Community Programme (later Employment Training) team. So far, this combination has seen major overhauls for the 'K1' and 'J72', the cosmetic restoration of Bittern as No 2509 Silver Link, the rebuilding of the 'Q6s' tender and, most significant of all, the total restoration of Blue Peter. Here, Blue Peter and 2005 are seen in the depot on track laid by ICI specially for the project from a connection on the works internal railway system. Also to be seen is a traction engine being overhauled by the CP scheme for Beamish Museum. ICI's contribution to NELPG's work in recent years cannot be overestimated. All those with an interest in the Group's locomotives have reason to be grateful to the firm for their wholehearted commitment to the Wilton project.**
Maurice Burns

Left: **In August 1990, another completed restoration comes off the production line! 901's overhaul took many years, not least because of the £50,000 which had to be raised to pay for the work. In the end the long wait to see this unique locomotive from the National Collection back in working order has been well worthwhile.**
Maurice Burns

5 ON THE MAIN LINE

For several years after the end of BR steam in 1968, the prospect of travelling behind main line steam seemed remote. Flying Scotsman was the only loco allowed to operate over BR and NELPG's first venture into main line specials in June 1969 was to be her last trip before leaving for the USA. Whilst Flying Scotsman was away, even that lifeline was gone. Light engine movements had to be performed in 'light steam' as locos were hauled around by diesels, although 2392 managed to break the rules when it steamed from Philadelphia to Thornaby via Newcastle Central in the spring of 1969. The return to steam came in June 1972 but at this time NELPG was not involved. The authorised list was targeted upon a few large main-line locos normally confined in depots, such as Tyseley and Hereford, where meaningful operations were not possible. It was the Stockton & Darlington 150th anniversary in 1975 which was to bring NELPG onto the scene.

The package of celebrations was to include main line running on the Esk Valley line from Battersby to Whitby and a number of locos were added to BR's approved list for the purpose of operating these trains. 2005 and 4767 were among them.

In the event, it was left to 2005 to power all of the special workings on the Esk Valley line that summer. Two incoming specials (including one for NELPG members from Newcastle) were hauled from Battersby to Whitby and return whilst another worked through from Whitby to Pickering.

Having gained coveted places on the list, NELPG was soon playing a full part as a member of the Steam Loco Operators Association, for some time the only member whose locos were based on an operating railway.

NELPG's operating base on the NYMR and the self-sufficient traditions of the Group meant that its attitude to operating specials was different from that of those owners whose locos were trapped in their depots. Many operators were pleased to accept hire fees which scarcely paid for fuel, simply in order to see their locos in action. But if NELPG ran a tour, it was to be for profits which could be ploughed back into the restoration of the Group's engines. The Group, assisted by the availability in Newcastle of high capacity tourist stock, was able to run highly profitable tours at competitive prices. The 1976 'Scarborough Flyer', with 12 coaches on the leg from York to Scarborough and return, carried 723 passengers, probably the highest total on any post-1968 railtour.

From small beginnings in 1975, NELPG's operations on the main line grew steadily with 4767 and 2005 taking their share of the railtour programme.

At first 4767 and 2005 were able to work only between Stockton and Newcastle via the Durham coast. Opportunities increased in 1980 when the Newcastle to Carlisle line was reopened to steam operations and several memorable tours were to follow, not least 2005's twin single-handed attacks on Ais Gill in 1983.

More recently, both engines have participated in Scotrail's highly successful Fort William-Mallaig operation, where 2005 in particular has excelled. The logistics of this operation should not be under-estimated. In 1990 NELPG has provided a support crew of up to four people to maintain and prepare the locomotive for 58 days of main line running. As if this were not enough, the Fort William base is several hundred miles from volunteers' homes and from the Group's stores and workshops. To provide volunteer transport to, from and around Fort William NELPG even operated its own company car (an elderly estate) for several years.

Since joining the main line pool, the 'K1' has made over 200 trips on the main line, amassing a total of more than 21,000 miles in the process with excellent reliability – a great credit to all those involved.

Left: The first revenue earning trip for a NELPG loco on BR metals took place on 8 June 1975, when 2005 hauled a through train from Whitby to Pickering. A week later it took over a Newcastle-Whitby tour organised by the Group from Battersby to Whitby and return. A feature of the arrangements was a midday short trip from Whitby to Glaisdale during the main special's layover period. 2005 is seen heading this train out of Whitby on the picturesque route beside the harbour. *John Hunt*

Top: A year later, in July 1976, NELPG organised a more ambitious railtour from Newcastle to Scarborough using 4767 down the Durham coast and Evening Star between York and Scarborough. On the return trip, 4767 is seen restarting the train from a rather sad looking Stockton station. *Peter J. Robinson*

Above: At the beginning of 1981, 4767 moved to Carnforth to allow it to participate in 'Cumbrian Mountain Express' working. On 4 April it started its return trip to the north east by piloting 5407 on a 13-coach train over the 'Long Drag'. This was the first double-header over the line since the famous 'Fifteen Guinea Special' in 1968 – BR's last steam-hauled train. The pair is seen here crossing Ribblehead Viaduct. *John Whiteley*

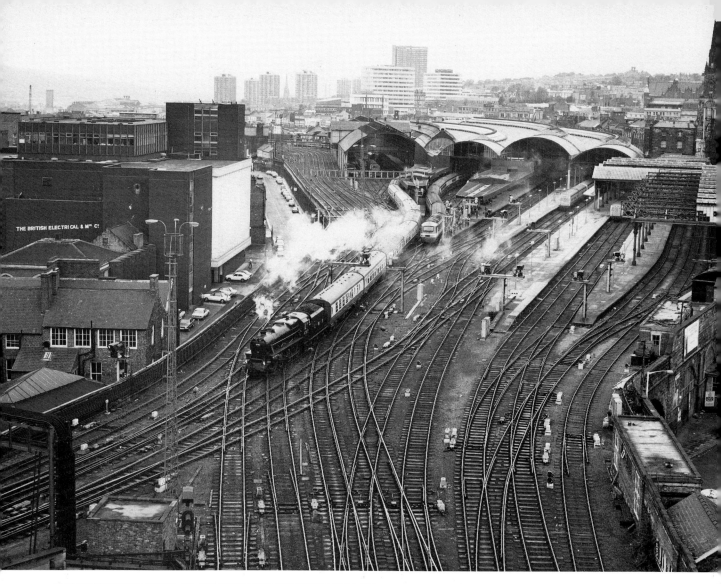

Left: June 1981 saw evidence of a new and more flexible attitude to railtour operation, when BR organised a shuttle service of special trains between Newcastle and Hexham to celebrate the bicentenary of the birth of George Stephenson. Not unreasonably, 4767 was the chosen locomotive. It is seen here, in the well known view from the castle keep, leaving for Hexham via the High Level Bridge and Dunston. *John Hunt*

Below left: To celebrate NELPG's 15th anniversary at the end of October 1981, 2005 and 4767 double-headed a railtour from Middlesbrough via Carlisle and on to Hellifield, allowing them to be transferred to Carnforth for 'Cumbrian Mountain Express' operations. The two are seen here leaving the west end of Newcastle and heading onto the (now closed) direct line to Blaydon. Both this crossing and that in the previous picture have since totally disappeared and the scene at the now electrified Newcastle Central is totally changed. Earlier in the journey, the train had been brought to a stand in Sunderland south tunnel. On restarting, 2005 slipped badly and brought a shower of filth onto the top of both engines, thus negating the hard work by volunteer cleaners prior to the trip! *John Hunt*

Right: In January 1983, 2005 was given the opportunity to tackle Ais Gill single-handed with the 'Northumbrian Mountain Pullman' from Middlesbrough. Soon after dawn, 2005 is seen crossing the Wear Bridge from Sunderland into Monkwearmouth. *John Hunt*

Below: Later in the day, 2005 breasts the last few yards of the climb to Ais Gill summit after the climb from Carlisle. With a heavy train, the 'K1' broke no records in its ascent from Appleby. But despite this, the train topped the summit in fine style – a rigorous test for a loco of the 'K1s' size. *John Hunt*

Left: **Later in 1983, 2005 had the opportunity to undertake some local runs in the north east on the occasion of the 150th anniversary of the opening of the first railway workshops at Shildon. Four return trips were operated between Middlesbrough and Shildon, 200 miles in total. 50mph running was necessary at times to keep up with the tight schedules. It was also a rare opportunity to see steam on the east coast main line, albeit only on the short stretch either side of Bank Top station in Darlington. 2005 is seen passing the site of Darlington motive power depot on the first of the day's trains to Shildon.** *John Hunt*

Below left: **August 1986 brought another opportunity for intensive workings on the home patch when 2005 worked a pair of 'Saltburn Express' trains from Newcastle to Saltburn and return. This 'local' operation required 240 miles of passenger haulage in one day together with considerable light engine mileage and was a remarkable achievement. The train is seen here passing the now demolished blast furnaces at Cargo Fleet.** *John Hunt*

SCOTLAND

Above: **George Stephenson was invited to participate in Scotrail's first season of Fort William-Mallaig steam operations in 1986. These daily 84 mile out and back steam workings required new levels of organisation and dedication. Loco owners undertake to provide their engines in steam and ready to run for BR footplate crews six days out of seven in each alternate week of the operation – quite a commitment so far from home. The engine is seen here on a Mallaig train near Beasdale.** *John Hunt*

Left: **After the main West Highland season, 44767 operated a number of other special trains in Scotland. At the beginning of September 1986, it took a train from Inverness to Helmsdale and return, the furthest north a steam engine has run since the return to steam. George Stephenson is seen here crossing the viaduct at Invershin.** *Maurice Burns*

Above: **2005 has had several summer seasons on the West Highland, a type of service where the engine is in its element. Here 2005 eases its train round the sharp curve of Glenfinnan viaduct.** *John Hunt*

Right: **2005 on the short but sharp climb into Glenfinnan station on a Mallaig-bound train in August 1987.** *Maurice Burns*

Above: On two occasions it has been possible to organise steam railtours in conjunction with 2005's return to the south. In November 1987 No 2005 and its train steam purposefully round Horseshoe Curve with snow-capped Beinn a' Chuirn in the distance as the train heads for Crianlarich and thence to Glasgow. *Ian Krause*

Right: A year later, weather on the return trip took a turn for the worse and much of 2005's journey took place in a blizzard. The train is seen here a mile north of Gorton. Ironically, the railtour had been at risk of cancellation due to fire risk only twenty four hours earlier! *John Hunt*

Below: Old and new on the east coast main line. After its sojourn at Keighley in March 1982, the 'K1' returned to the NYMR via York. Here it collected 2392 which had been on display in the National Railway Museum and the assembly set off up the East Coast main line at lunchtime on 29 March. At the London-Edinburgh half way point near Beningborough the two locomotives were overhauled by a High Speed Train – and the photographer nearly missed a classic shot! *John Hunt*

6 COUNTRYWIDE TRAVELS

In the atmosphere of BR's steam ban from 1968 onwards, Group members never dared raise their ambitions beyond operation on the NYMR. With the potential of an 18-mile run, this has always been a perfectly acceptable aim. The opportunity to embark upon mainline railtours in 1975 saw ventures further afield. In recent years, NELPG's engines have increasingly found themselves in destinations never dreamed of in those early days, sometimes as a consequence of railtour operations, at other times, on specific visits to help out or participate in events at other steam railway sites.

Several factors have led to the increase in these travels. Firstly, the cost of road transport by low-loader has fallen, relative to the income an engine can generate and most lines are now able to offload locomotives delivered by road. Secondly, the need to bring in outside motive power, either to counter shortages or to offer something new, has increased. Perhaps just as important, today's more stringent

gulations which require boiler lifts at regular intervals, drive owners to find as much work for their engines as possble whilst they have valid boiler ertificates.

This new factor in managing a steam ocomotive fleet has seen NELPG's ngines in operation or on display at a ozen different locations apart from hose encountered in main line railurs.

eft: The 'J27's' initial restoration was started at hornaby but ICI provided premises for its completion at the loco depot within their Billingham orks. In October 1971 the work was completed nd the opportunity was taken during a steam st to recreate a scene which could have been een 50 years before. 2392, resplendent in NER very, shunted 600 tons of internal coal traffic at illingham, much of it in elderly secondhand ER coal wagons. *John Hunt*

elow left: Six years later, the time had come for a tubing operation on 2392. It was not likely to come to the top of the priority list for some time and a temporary home was needed until Deviation Shed could be built. The situation was resolved for NELPG by the National Railway useum, which also had a problem. With its own xamples on loan elsewhere, the NRM found self without that most typical part of the British ailway scene, the 0-6-0 goods locomotive. To fill he gap, 2392 went on show in the museum in ecember 1977 and remained there for more than our years, the first privately owned loco to be isplayed there for any length of time. *John Hunt*

Above: In March 1982, after a round of railtour duty, 2005 was able to spend the Enthusiasts' Weekend on the Keighley & Worth Valley Railway working, amongst other things, a non-stop Keighley to Oxenhope train. On 28 March, 2005 is seen crossing Mytholmes viaduct with a photographers' special – a train of parcels vans for Oxenhope. *John Hunt*

Below: When Bittern came into the Group's care, the problem arose as to how best to employ it. A badly cracked frame and three other 'A4s' in working order meant that it was not likely to be a priority for restoration. Then the forthcoming

anniversary of Mallard's world record breaking run brought inspiration. At Wilton, the engine had its full prewar streamlining restored and it was repainted in the distinctive silver grey livery of the earliest members of the class as a replica of the prototype, No 2509, Silver Link. On 2 July 1988, the spectacular sight of three 'A4s' was to be seen at the National Railway Museum, when Mallard, the new Silver Link and Sir Nigel Gresley lined up outside the museum. Silver Link spent the summer on display at York before being moved to the Stephenson Museum in North Tyneside, where it remains on public view. *Maurice Burns*

Above: **When the 'J72' was acquired, there was some concern that it would never be able to earn its keep and that it would be a drain on resources required for NELPG's other locos. Nothing could have proved further from the truth! In the peak season, the growing length of trains and inadequate run round facilities at Grosmont created the need for a station pilot. Such work was to keep the engine gainfully employed for several years until the extension of Grosmont loop in 1989. It has also shown its ability to work in tandem with other locos on through services to Pickering.**

More recently, the engine's small size and its

unique combination of power, attractiveness and popularity has led to an ever growing demand for its use elsewhere. It spent the summer of 1988 on the Yorkshire Dales Railway at Embsay. On its return journey 69023 made a diversion so that it could put in an appearance at a Hartlepool nuclear power station open day, where it provided cab rides. It returned in 1989 and is seen here dwarfed by the power station buildings. *Maurice Burns*

Above right: **In spring 1989, came another change of scene for Joem when it spent a few months at the Didcot home of the Great Western Society.**

Here it is seen in the august company of, amongst others, Duke of Gloucester and City of Truro. Beside the former, Joem's diminutive stature is particularly apparent. *Maurice Burns*

Right: **Whilst Joem performed in Oxfordshire, th 'J27' was returning to one of the traditional haunts of its class. In June 1989, 2392 made its debut at the Stephenson Railway Museum on the former Metro Test Track between Shiremoor and Percy Main in Tyne and Wear. Here it joined Bittern/Silver Link already on static display. Or 11 June 2392 is seen on a demonstration freig train south of Shiremoor.** *Maurice Burns*

Right: **During its sojourn at Didcot, the North Norfolk Railway found itself with a motive power crisis. Instead of returning to the north east, Joem was conveyed to Sheringham where it operated for the remainder of the summer season. 69023 is seen here in July 1989 passing Wensum Junction box in company with one of the line's resident locomotives, on a train bound for Weybourne.** *Maurice Burns*

Centre right: **Joem returned to Grosmont in the autumn of 1989 but spring 1990 saw it on the road again. For 12 months from April 1990, 69023 operated most of the East Somerset Railway's services during a motive power shortage on that line. It is seen here breasting the summit of the line on a train from Mendip Vale to East Cranmore in April 1990.** *Maurice Burns*

Below: **After its overhaul at the Stephenson Railway Centre, the 'P3' spent a season in the second half of 1990 working on the Keighley & Worth Valley Railway. Here it was able to be run in thoroughly whilst performing useful work on this busy five-mile line. Whilst at Keighley 2392 was given the honour of commissioning the line's newly installed turntable, moved to the line from Garsdale on the Settle and Carlisle line.** *Maurice Burns*